The Sculptors of Light

poems about Cuban women artists

written by **Margarita Engle**

illustrated by **Cecilia Puglesi**

Reycraft Books
145 Huguenot Street
New Rochelle, NY 10801

reycraftbooks.com

Reycraft Books is a trade imprint and trademark of Newmark Learning, LLC.

Library of Congress Control Number: 2023902962

Hardcover ISBN: 978-1-4788-7960-2
Paperback ISBN: 978-1-4788-7961-9

Author photo: Courtesy of Shevaun Williams
Illustrator photo: Courtesy of Ramón López Seco de Herrera

Printed in Dongguan, China. 8557/0523/20217
10 9 8 7 6 5 4 3 2 1

First Edition published by Reycraft Books 2023.

For Izabella, Maya, and other girls who love to create.

Acknowledgments

I thank God for art, my family for love,

my friends for encouragement,

my agent Michelle Humphrey,

my editor, the illustrator,

and the whole publishing team.

DEAR READERS/QUERIDOS LECTORES,

Many of the artists in this book are just as celebrated in Cuba and the Cuban American community as Frida Kahlo is in Mexico and the Mexican American community or Georgia O'Keefe in the U.S. Southwest. Never let anyone convince you there is no room for more women artists from every country and every culture. When you create something beautiful, sign your name!

Your friend/Tu amiga,
Margarita Engle

ANONYMOUS

For thousands of years, Indigenous women and girls
on the island called Cuba, wove cotton, carved wood, shaped clay,
and made feather capes, coral bracelets, sea shell decorations, and
painted suns, moons, and spiral hurricanes, circles within circles,
human faces, and other powerful shapes that can still be seen today
on cave walls or scraped onto stone figurines.

For hundreds of years, women and girls with Taíno and Ciboney
ancestors have blended Native skills with arts from Spain, Africa, and
China to make objects of grace and strength. It's often impossible to say
whether lace, embroidery, or ceramics were made by one artisan or
another, because names were not signed, fame was not claimed, and
men called the art of their wives and daughters by smaller labels:
handicrafts, tradition, folk art, women's work...

but now isn't it finally time to sign our names within the designs
so that we will be remembered as true artists who portray
our world in unique ways?

Historical Note

Cuba's "folk art," like the population, is a combination of Indigenous, Spanish, West African, and Chinese elements. When my mother was growing up in the town of Trinidad, lacemaking and embroidery were skills all girls learned at home and in Catholic schools. She has fond memories of decorating baby clothes for canastillas, gift baskets presented to each newborn, with needlework contributed by many women. As a teenager, she studied art, touched up the colors of portraits in her uncle's photography studio, and painted designs on Trinidad's distinctive yellow clay ceramics. Trinidad is now a UNESCO World Heritage Site and a World Craft City, the abundance of handmade lace recognized as an artwork made by thousands of women. Many still do not sign their names and never receive recognition for their individual skills and accomplishments.

Poetic Form

Prose poem (long lines) with assonance (vowel rhymes)

AMELIA'S GARDEN

Amelia Peláez
(1896–1968)

Amelia's life began in a quiet town
where, along with all her sisters and brothers,
she learned painting, poetry, and other ways
to celebrate peace, because Cuba's long wars
for independence from Spain were finally over.

Just when she was learning to expect happiness
her father fell ill, and the family moved to Havana
where even the best doctors could not save him.

At first, Amelia's grief was fierce
but eventually, she found comfort in the garden
of fragrant orchids and fruit trees, where she painted
golden pineapples, orange mangos, pink cactus fruit,
a fish on a red plate, and a blue tablecloth

with embroidery
swirled along the edges
of soothing blue cloth.

Amelia studied, traveled, and exhibited her work,
then returned to the garden in Cuba, where she became
one of the most famous women artists, her stained glass colors
overlapping like the patterns of nature,

petals
leaves,
and teardrops
arranged like brilliant
sun rays.

Historical Note

Amelia Peláez del Casal is one of the best-known Cuban artists. She was born in Yaguajay, Cuba, in 1896. When her father was sick, the family moved to Havana. After his death, Amelia painted in the garden of her new home. There, she began to develop her distinctive style of brilliantly colored still-life paintings and portraits that resemble the stained glass windows of old Cuban houses.

With the help of government grants, she studied art in Cuba, New York, and France, at a time when few women were accepted into the art world. After visiting Spain and Italy, she exhibited in Paris, then returned to the island, where once again, she painted in the garden of her childhood home. She also created murals, such as the one at the Habana Libre Hotel. She died in Havana in 1968, but her work can still be seen at the Museo Nacional de Bellas Artes, La Habana, and the Museum of Modern Art in New York.

Poetic Form

Free verse (no meter or rhyme) with assonance (vowel rhymes) and alliteration (words that start with the same letter)

GALAXIES

Loló Soldevilla
(1901–1971)

As a child, Loló played violin
and performed with orchestras.
When music took her traveling, she was alone
in hotel rooms, where she taught herself to paint
rhythms, dots, triangles,
all the sights of art
and sounds of instruments
                    mixed together
                            as she listened to symphonies
while striking a slab of wood
                    with her feathery
paintbrush.

                            Experiment!
                She transformed melodies
                    into bright spheres
                            until
her work
began to claim the shapes
of   stars   constellations   planets
circles
        and
            lines
                gliding
                        across
            museum
    walls
            a musical
                        universe
                                mysteries
                                    orbiting.

Historical Note

Loló Soldevilla Nieto was born in Pinar del Río and grew up in Havana, where she played violin and sang with an all-female orchestra. Jailed several times for demonstrating against the dictators Machado in Cuba and Franco in Spain, she did not begin to sculpt and paint until she was living in Paris many years later. Her abstract geometric patterns grew from the visual rhythms of music as well as a fascination with the movements of celestial bodies in the universe. Soldevilla died in Cuba in 1971. Recently, international exhibits have revived interest in her work.

Poetic Form

Free verse (no meter or rhyme) and concrete (shaped like the subject matter)

THE EARLY WOMEN PHOTOGRAPHERS OF CUBA

nameless for so long
they emerge from history
clearly visible

Historical Note

The 1899 census listed only seven female photographers in Cuba. By the middle of the twentieth century, there were still only a few dozen. At first, most were known by the names of their famous photographer husbands, even though they shared the same cameras. Photos by la viuda de Gregorio Casañas were published in 1909, her name reduced to "the widow of Gregorio Casañas." Ulderica Mañas y Parejeon (1905-1985) used her own name when she represented Cuba as part of the United Nations Commission on the Status of Women in 1953, documenting the poverty of street vendors in Peru. A catalogue of Cuban women photographers is now being compiled and documented by art historian Aldeide Delgado, whose work has been published in Cuban Art News.org

Poetic Form

Haiku, with a syllable count of 5-7-5

THE SCULPTOR OF LIGHT

Rita Longa
(1912–2000)

Art school helped Rita get started
but she was self-taught too, carving marble,
casting bronze, and making tile mosaics
as she explored the clear spaces
between solid shapes.

Screams.
Thirst.
Dreams.
Any word could be shown as an emotional form
in metal or stone, human or animal, a graceful swan
or a family of deer as they climbed a rocky slope
antlers
and ears
touching
sky.

Statues of dancers seemed to twirl
stone arms reaching—ballerina and rumbera
two equally beautiful movements.

Rita chose a town
and filled it with sculptures.

She chose a swamp, and created images
of Taíno villagers, women, men, girls, and boys
who farm, weave, sing, and shape clay
in the old ways, a reminder that we
can still treasure
the skills
of our ancestors.

Historical Note

Rita Longa Arostegui was born in Havana in 1912 and died there in 2000. Primarily self-taught, she sculpted marble, tile, and bronze. Outside the Havana Zoo, a family of sculpted deer climbs a hill. In front of the art museum, a modernist sculpture titled Shape, Space, and Light has become one of the best-known statues in Cuba. Longa turned the small town of Las Tunas into the "City of Sculpture" by erecting so many statues that it became an attraction. Twenty-five images of Indigenous villagers in the Zapata Swamp are a beloved tribute to Cuba's Taíno roots. Longa is the island's most famous sculptor.

Poetic Form

Free verse (no meter or end rhymes) with some internal rhyme (within lines)

Historical Note

Carmen Herrera was born in Havana and has lived in the U.S. since the 1950s. As the youngest of seven children in a crowded home, she learned to value quiet simplicity. She worked in obscurity for much of her youth, rejected by galleries and museums because she was female and an immigrant. At the age of 89, she finally sold a painting. Her work is now highly valued and has been collected by the Museum of Modern Art in New York, the Tate Modern in London, and the Hirshhorn Museum in Washington D.C. In 2019, when she was 104, New York City exhibited five of her sculptures outdoors.

Poetic Form

Tanka, with a syllable count of 5-7-5-7-7

MINIMALIST

Carmen Herrera
(1915–2022)

decades of patience
her quest for the stark beauty
of simplicity
straight lines—bold colors that reach
a bright sky of surprises

BUILDING HOPE

María Margarita Egaña Fernández
(1921–1975)

A woman architect? Men say
my dream of building homes is strange,
but I think it's time for a change.
I design parks where children play,
surrounded by houses where rays
of sunlight shimmer, a breeze flows
between layers of glazed windows,
flat roofs rest against sturdy beams,
and nature makes everything seem
hopeful, so families can grow.

Historical Note

María Margarita Egaña Fernández was born in Havana, where she studied architecture. She married another architect and moved to the city of Santiago, where she developed her own style, becoming a pioneer of the Modernist movement. The homes she designed were built around shared green areas. Visual effects such as embedded beams and glazed windows created a sense of connection to nature. After the Cuban revolution Egaña moved to Puerto Rico.

Poetic Form

Traditional Cuban décima of ten octosyllabic lines, with the rhyme pattern abba ac cddc

NANCY'S WINGS

Nancy Morejón
(1944–present)

From poverty to poetry,
jazz and rumba, music, verses,
prizes, travel, honors, paintings,
success in every art she tries,
inspiration for brave young girls
Afrocubana feminist.

Historical Note

Nancy Morejón was born in Havana, where she became the first
Afro-Cuban student to receive a degree in the arts from the University
of Havana and the first Afro-Cuban woman to receive Cuba's National
Prize for Literature. While she is primarily known as a highly respected
poet, she travels widely, lectures, teaches, translates, and experiments
with visual arts such as painting.

Poetic Form

Blank verse (metered, unrhymed) and list poem (listing many aspects
of one subject)

EARTH-BODY

Ana Mendieta
(1948–1985)

Ana's art was her own human shape
outlines of mud, sand, grass, leaves
pressed onto walls or green earth
helping her feel closer
to nature, so she
could remember
her island
Cuba
home.

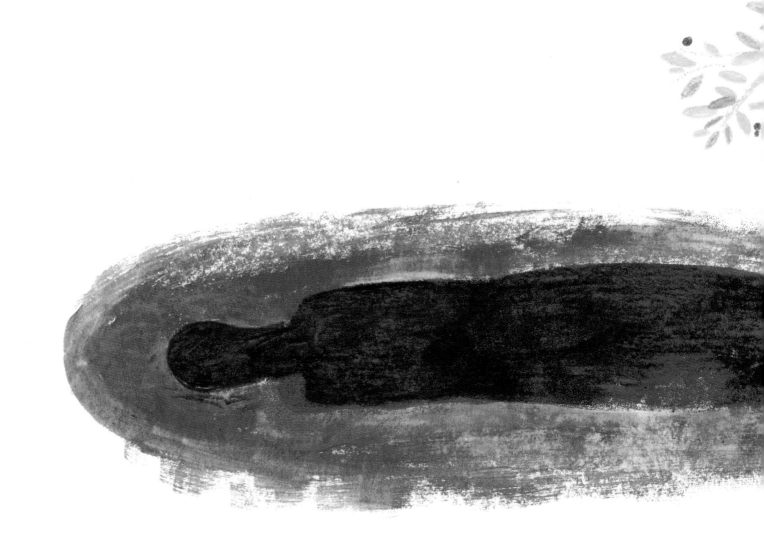

Historical Note

Ana Mendieta was a "Pedro Pan" child, sent away from Cuba at the age of 12, along with her 14-year-old sister. The girls were housed in refugee camps, institutions, and foster homes in the U.S., before finally being reunited with their parents. Mendieta studied at the University of Iowa, then traveled and became known for her unique performance art installations, with themes of connection to the earth, a sense of belonging, and violence against women. She died in New York after falling from a window under suspicious circumstances. Mendieta is one of the best-known Cuban-American women artists, widely respected for the bold feminist aspects of her work.

Poetic Form

Nonet of nine lines with the number of syllables decreasing from nine tone

Historical Note

Belkis Ayón was the first internationally known Afro-Cuban woman artist. She defied cultural traditions by using her printmaking skills to create towering, mouthless figures that altered stories from the secret, all-male religious society called Abakuá. Using a process called collography, her prints were textured with sandpaper, cloth, string, leaves, and grass.

Poetic Form

Haiku sequence, each haiku with a syllable count of 5-7-5

NEVER SILENCED

Belkis Ayón
(1967–1999)

heroic legends
only the men had voices
until she painted

people with no mouths
black, white, gray, or vibrant hues
old stories made new

FREEDOM OF SPEECH

Many artists

Artists are outspoken opponents of censorship.
When one is arrested for speaking out bravely
she sets an example for others
who paint
sculpt
weave
dance
write
shout
pleas for freedom
to speak freely.

Historical Note

On July 11, 2021, many young protesters were arrested for peacefully demanding
the release of imprisoned artists whose work was regarded by the government
as dangerous because it expressed the need for artistic freedom. Some of those
dissident artists are men. Others are women. Some, such as Tania Bruguera, are
world-famous. Others are not widely known outside Cuba. All were united under the
peaceful slogan, Patria y Vida (Homeland and Life), which rejects the government's
war slogan Patria o Muerte (Homeland or Death).

Poetic Form

Free verse

SELECTED FURTHER READING

Amelia Peláez

Alonso, Alejandro G., Amelia Peláez, La Habana: Editorial Letras
Cubanas, 1988.

Loló Soldevilla

Grove, Jeffrey, editor; Loló Soldevilla, Berlin: Hatje Cantz, 2019

Early Photographers

www.CubanArtNews.org/2017/01/19/Uncovering-a-hidden-history-
women-photographers-in-Cuba

Rita Longa

Alonso, Alejancro G., La obra escultórica de Rita Longa,
La Habana: Editorial Letras Cubanas, 1998.

Carmen Herrera

www.TheArtStory.org/CarmenHerrera

Ana Mendieta

www.TheArtStory.org/AnaMendieta

María Margarita Egaña Hernández

www.vitruvius.com/br/revistas/read/arquitextos/058.09:VistaAlegre

Nancy Morejón

Morejón, Nancy, Looking Within/Mirar adentro, Detroit: Wayne State
University Press, 2003.

Belkis Ayón

www.ayonbelkis.cult.cu

MARGARITA ENGLE

is the Cuban-American author of many verse novels, memoirs, and picture books, including *The Surrender Tree*, *Enchanted Air*, *Drum Dream Girl*, and *Dancing Hands*. Awards include a Newbery Honor, Pura Belpré, Golden Kite, Walter, Jane Addams, PEN U.S.A., and NSK Neustadt, among others. Margarita served as the national 2017-2019 Young People's Poet Laureate. She is a three-time U.S. nominee for the Astrid Lindgren Book Award. Her most recent books are *Your Heart, My Sky*, *A Song of Frutas*, *Light for All*, *Rima's Rebellion*, and *Singing With Elephants*. Margarita was born in Los Angeles, but developed a deep attachment to her mother's homeland during childhood summers with relatives on the island. She studied agronomy, botany, and creative writing, and now lives in central California with her husband.

CECILIA PUGLESI

was born in Mendoza, Argentina, where she first studied agronomy, then later design. She got her master's degree in Barcelona and, with a Fulbright grant, she got her MFA in Computer Art at the School of Visual Arts in New York City. Her graduation short film allowed her to travel around the world, where she won several international awards. She has worked in Spain, Austria, Ireland, New York City, and Paris, where she lives with her lovely family and works in animation and as an illustrator.